I'll Throw the Book at You, BEETLE BAILEY

Here's another in the happy series of books based on one of the most famous comic strips in the country. Once again the madcap inmates of Camp Swampy valiantly strive to overcome their own ineptitude—and succeed in delighting us on every page.

Mort Walker again gives us a barrel of laughs in his marvelous cartoons concerning the most unprofessional soldier in the army!

I'll throw the book at you,

beetle bailey

ACE TEMPO BOOKS, NEW YORK

An Ace Tempo Original

ISBN: 0-448-12635-4

This Printing: August 1982

Tempo Books is registered in the United States Patent Office

Published simultaneously in Canada

Manufactured in the United States of America

MORT
WALKER

I HOPE YOU WEREN'T TOO ROUGH ON BEETLE, SARGE

HE WAS SMILING WHEN I LEFT HIM, SIR

10-19

WHY IS OTTO SALUTING THAT GARBAGE CAN?

MORT WALKER

9-26

3-22

10-6

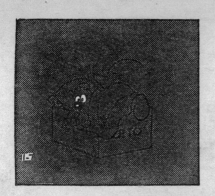

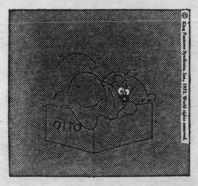

OH-OH!

GOLF! GOLF! GOLF! THAT'S ALL YOU THINK OF! GET BACK IN THE HOUSE AND THINK OF SOMETHING ELSE!

1-30

10-22

3-28

HAVE YOU SEEN THE GENERAL'S NEW SUPER SWIVEL CHAIR?

Mort Walker

THAT WAS THE LIEUTENANT'S FIRST SPEECH BEFORE AN AUDIENCE

AS FAR AS I'M CONCERNED, IT'S ALSO HIS LAST.

4-1

MORT WALKER